BIRDS
Play Tricks!

BY JUDY THORPE

ANIMAL TRICKSTERS

 Gareth Stevens
PUBLISHING

Please visit our website, www.garethstevens.com. For a free color catalog of all our high-quality books, call toll free 1-800-542-2595 or fax 1-877-542-2596.

Library of Congress Cataloging-in-Publication Data

Names: Thorpe, Judy, author.
Title: Birds play tricks! / Judy Thorpe.
Description: Buffalo, NY : Gareth Stevens Publishing, [2025] | Series: Animal tricksters | Includes index.
Identifiers: LCCN 2023033168 | ISBN 9781538293461 (library binding) | ISBN 9781538293454 (paperback) | ISBN 9781538293478 (ebook)
Subjects: LCSH: Birds–Behavior–Juvenile literature. | Birds–Juvenile literature.
Classification: LCC QL676.2 .T567 2025 | DDC 598.15–dc23/eng/20230818
LC record available at https://lccn.loc.gov/2023033168

Published in 2025 by
Gareth Stevens Publishing
2544 Clinton Street
Buffalo, NY 14224

Designer: Andrea Davison-Bartolotta
Editor: Jennifer Lombardo

Photo credits: Cover, pp. 1, 11 John Navajo/Shutterstock.com; series art (background texture) Kriangkrai Namtongbai/Shutterstock.com; series art (feather texture) speedphoto/Shutterstock.com; p. 4 ledokolua/Shutterstock.com; p. 5 BlueRingMedia/Shutterstock.com; p. 7 (bird) Dave Montreuil/Shutterstock.com; p. 7 (jackal) Henk Bogaard/Shutterstock.com; p. 8 Artush/Shutterstock.com; p. 9 Ishor gurung/Shutterstock.com; p. 13 Bruce MacQueen/Shutterstock.com; p. 15 (crow) DKeith/Shutterstock.com; p. 15 (raven) Piotr Krzeslak/Shutterstock.com; p. 16 © Yi-Kai Tea/iNaturalist.com; p. 17 Jean-Paul Ferrero/Auscape International Pty Ltd/Alamy Stock Photo; pp. 18, 19 Uwe Bergwitz/Shutterstock.com; p. 20 Naaman Abreu/Shutterstock.com; p. 21 Agnieszka Bacal/Shutterstock.com.

Some of the images in this book illustrate individuals who are models. The depictions do not imply actual situations or events.

Printed in the United States of America

CPSIA compliance information: Batch #CSGS25: For further information contact Gareth Stevens at 1-800-542-2595.

Find us on

CONTENTS

Tricky Birds. 4

The Fork-Tailed Drongo 6

A Food Thief. 8

The Cuckoo 10

The Green Heron 12

The New Caledonian Crow 14

Building and Planning 16

The Great Potoo 18

The Hummingbird. 20

Glossary. 22

For More Information 23

Index 24

Words in the glossary appear in **bold** type the first time they are used in the text.

TRICKY BIRDS

All around the world, there are birds with smart survival tricks. Sometimes they play these tricks to get away from danger. Other times, they trick their **prey** into coming close enough to get caught. Some even trick other birds!

Not all birds have the same tricks. Some make sounds that fool other animals. Others have feathers that help them blend into their **environment**. This trick is called camouflage. A few birds use tools. These tricky birds are very smart!

FUN FACT
All birds alive today are descended from dinosaurs!

CLASSIFICATION OF VERTEBRATES

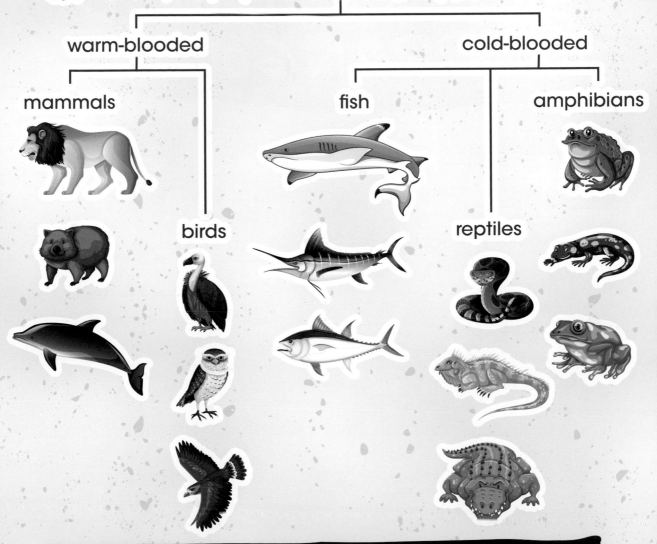

warm-blooded

cold-blooded

mammals

fish

amphibians

birds

reptiles

Birds are warm-blooded vertebrates, or animals with a backbone. Warm-blooded means their body stays at one temperature, no matter how hot or cold it is outside.

THE FORK-TAILED DRONGO

Most animals have special calls they make to warn each other of danger. When an animal hears this call, it knows it's time to leave! The fork-tailed drongo is a bird that's native to some parts of Africa. It knows how to **mimic** the calls of other animals.

Some drongos can make between 30 and 50 different calls. Some of the animals they can mimic are mongooses, jackals, and meerkats. Drongos also have their own calls they use to warn other drongos of real danger.

A type of wild dog called a jackal is one of the animals a drongo can mimic.

JACKAL

DRONGO

FUN FACT

Drongos sit high up in the trees, so it's easy for them to spot predator birds. For this reason, other kinds of birds use drongos as lookouts. They fly away when a drongo makes its real warning call.

A FOOD THIEF

When a drongo sees an animal eating something tasty, it makes a call. Sometimes it mimics the animal's own warning call. Other times, it mimics a predator's call. When the animal runs or flies away, the drongo flies down and takes the food!

Drongos learn a lot of different calls to stop other animals from getting too used to its mimicked calls. This is also why drongos sometimes mimic warning calls when another animal's predator is nearby.

Drongos are small, but they'll go after much larger birds to steal their food!

FUN FACT

Scientists who studied the drongo found that it could get 20 to 25 percent of its food by tricking other animals!

9

THE CUCKOO

One of the most famous bird tricksters is the cuckoo. Most birds build a nest to lay their eggs in, but not the cuckoo! A mother cuckoo lays an egg in another bird's nest. When the cuckoo **hatches**, it pushes all the other eggs out of the nest.

Without other babies around, the newly hatched cuckoo gets all the food its **foster** mother brings back to the nest. Most of the time, the foster mother doesn't figure out the cuckoo isn't its own baby.

A cuckoo baby may grow to be much bigger than its foster mother, but the mother still feeds it!

THE GREEN HERON

Green herons live mainly on the southeast and southwest coasts of North America. They make their nest near bodies of water such as lakes and ponds. They eat the animals that live in or near the water, such as small fish, frogs, worms, and mice.

Green herons sometimes use a trick to **lure** fish toward them. They break sticks into very small pieces and drop them in the water. To a fish, the sticks look like food. When they try to catch the "food," the heron catches them!

This green heron is looking for prey.

13

THE NEW CALEDONIAN CROW

Two other birds that use tools to catch prey are the crow and the raven. These belong to a very smart family of birds called corvids.

One kind of crow is the New Caledonian crow. It's native to a group of islands, called New Caledonia, near Australia. This crow is one of the smartest birds in the world. If it sees food floating out of reach in a **container** of water, it will drop a rock into the water. This moves the water up so the crow can reach the food.

RAVEN

CROW

Ravens and crows look almost the same,
but ravens are bigger. They also have
fluffy feathers near their throat.

15

BUILDING AND PLANNING

Scientists have seen New Caledonian crows make tools out of small sticks. They can bend the stick to make a hook. This lets them get into places that are hard to reach with just their beak. They use the hook to pull out the bugs they eat.

New Caledonian crows also know how to make plans. They can think about the steps they need to take to do something before they start the task. This is very unusual for an animal!

This New Caledonian crow is using a
stick to get a bug out of the log.

THE GREAT POTOO

The great potoo is a very unusual bird. It's sometimes called the "ghost bird" because not many people have seen one in person. At least, many people don't know they've seen one! Great potoos are so good at camouflage that they're almost **invisible**.

Great potoos are nocturnal. This means they sleep during the day and hunt at night. Their camouflage keeps them safe while they sleep. The color of their feathers helps them blend in with, or hide in, the trees they sleep in.

From far away, this great potoo looks like another branch.

THE HUMMINGBIRD

A mother bird and its eggs are very **vulnerable** because they can't move away from danger. Birds must hide their nest and eggs! Hummingbirds are especially good at this.

A hummingbird makes its nest with dandelion down, or fluff. It sticks the down together with something sticky, such as spiderwebs. Hummingbirds are good at shaping the nest so it looks like part of the branch it's on. Finally, a mother hummingbird camouflages the nest by sticking **lichens** to the outside. This keeps the hummingbird's eggs safe until they hatch. What a neat trick!

If there were no birds in this nest,
it would be nearly invisible.

21

GLOSSARY

container: An object used to hold something.

descend: To come from an animal of an earlier time.

environment: The natural world in which a plant or animal lives.

foster: A parent that raises a child they did not give birth to.

hatch: To break open or come out of.

invisible: Unable to be seen.

lichen: A gray, green, or yellow plantlike organism made up of a fungus and an alga, and often appearing in flat patches on rocks.

lure: To draw an animal closer in order to catch it.

mimic: To copy.

prey: An animal that is hunted by other animals for food.

vulnerable: In an unsafe position.

Books

Barnes, Rachael. *Hummingbirds*. Minneapolis, MN: Bellwether Media, 2023.

Sibley, David. *What It's Like to Be a Bird, Adapted for Young Readers*. New York, NY: Delacorte Press, 2023.

Sprott, Gary. *Crows Hate People! And Other Strange Facts*. Vero Beach, FL: High Tide, 2020.

Websites

Active Wild: Raven Facts
www.activewild.com/raven
Read more about ravens.

BrainPOP: All About Bird Anatomy
www.brainpop.com/games/allaboutbirdanatomy
Build your own bird in this fun online game.

Fact Animal: Potoo Facts
www.factanimal.com/potoo
Learn more about the amazing great potoo, including what its call sounds like.

INDEX

baby birds, 10, 11

call, 4, 6, 7, 8, 17

camouflage, 4, 18, 19, 20, 21

cuckoo, 10, 11

dinosaur, 4

eggs, 5, 10, 20

feathers, 15

fork-tailed drongo, 6, 7, 8, 9

great potoo, 18, 19

green heron, 12, 13

hummingbird, 20, 21

nest, 10, 11, 12, 20, 21

New Caledonian crow, 14, 15, 16, 17

raven, 14, 15

tools, 4, 12, 14, 16, 17

vertebrate, 5